THE STORY OF
THE OTHER WISE MAN

HENRY VAN DYKE

*I saw him moving among the
throngs of men in populous Egypt*

The Story of
THE OTHER WISE MAN

By

HENRY VAN DYKE

Author of "The Mansion" "The Lost Boy"
"The Child Christ in Art" Etc.

With Many Drawings
in Color and Line by
J. R. FLANAGAN

Harper & Brothers Publishers
New York and London

CONTENTS

ILLUSTRATIONS

Who seeks for heaven alone to save his soul,
May keep the path, but will not reach the goal;
While he who walks in love may wander far,
Yet God will bring him where the blessed are.

PREFACE

IT is now some years since this little story was set afloat on the sea of books. It is not a man-of-war, nor even a high-sided merchant-man; only a small, peaceful sailing-vessel. Yet it has had rather an adventurous voyage. Twice it has fallen into the hands of pirates. The tides have carried it to far countries. It has been passed through the translator's port of entry into German, French, Armenian, Turkish, and perhaps some other foreign regions. Once I caught sight of it flying the outlandish flag of a brand-new phonetic language along the coasts of France; and once it was claimed by a dealer in antiquities as a long-lost legend of the Orient. Best of all, it has slipped quietly into many a far-away harbor that I have never seen, and found a kindly welcome, and brought back messages of good cheer from unknown friends.

Now it has turned home to be new-rigged and fitted for further voyaging. Before it is sent out again I have been asked to tell where the story came from and what it means.

I do not know where it came from—out of the air, perhaps. One thing is certain, it is not written in any other book, nor is it to be found among the ancient lore of the East. And yet I have never felt as if it were my own. It was a gift. It was sent to me; and it seemed as if I knew the Giver, though His name was not spoken.

The year had been full of sickness and sorrow. Every day brought trouble. Every night was tormented with pain. They are very long —those nights when one lies awake, and hears the laboring heart pumping wearily at its task, and watches for the morning, not knowing whether it will ever dawn. They are not nights of fear; for the thought of death grows strangely familiar when you have lived with it for a year. Besides, after a time you come to feel like a soldier who has been long standing still under fire; any change would be a relief. But they are lonely nights; they are

very heavy nights.   And their heaviest burden
is this:

You must face the thought that your work
in the world may be almost ended, but you
know that it is not nearly finished.

You have not solved the problems that per-
plexed you.   You have not reached the goal
that you aimed at.   You have not accomplished
the great task that you set for yourself.   You
are still on the way; and perhaps your journey
must end now,—nowhere,—in the dark.

Well, it was in one of these long lonely
nights that this story came to me. I had studied
and loved the curious tales of the Three Wise
Men of the East as they are told in the "Golden
Legend" of Jacobus de Voragine and other
medieval books.   But of the Fourth Wise Man
I had never heard until that night.   Then I
saw him distinctly, moving through the shadows in a little circle of light. His countenance
was as clear as the memory of my father's face
as I saw it for the last time a few months before.
The narrative of his journeyings and trials and
disappointments ran without a break.   Even
certain sentences came to me complete and

unforgetable, clear-cut like a cameo. All that I had to do was to follow Artaban, step by step, as the tale went on, from the beginning to the end of his pilgrimage.

Perhaps this may explain some things in the story. I have been asked many times why I made the Fourth Wise Man tell a lie, in the cottage at Bethlehem, to save the little child's life.

I did not make him tell a lie.

What Artaban said to the soldiers he said for himself, because he could not help it.

Is a lie ever justifiable? Perhaps not. But may it not sometimes seem inevitable?

And if it were a sin, might not a man confess it, and be pardoned for it more easily than for the greater sin of spiritual selfishness, or indifference, or the betrayal of innocent blood? That is what I saw Artaban do. That is what I heard him say. All through his life he was trying to do the best that he could. It was not perfect. But there are some kinds of failure that are better than success.

Though the story of the Fourth Wise Man came to me suddenly and without labor, there

was a great deal of study and toil to be done
before it could be written down. An idea
arrives without effort; a form can only be
wrought out by patient labor. If your story is
worth telling, you ought to love it enough to
be willing to work over it until it is true—true
not only to the ideal, but true also to the real.
The light is a gift; but the local color can only
be seen by one who looks for it long and steadily.
Artaban went with me while I toiled through a
score of volumes of ancient history and travel.
I saw his figure while I journeyed on the motionless sea of the desert and in the strange cities
of the East.

And now that his story is told, what does it
mean?

How can I tell? What does life mean? If
the meaning could be put into a sentence
there would be no need of telling the story.

Henry van Dyke.

You know the story of the Three Wise Men of the East, and how they traveled from far away to offer their gifts at the manger-cradle in Bethlehem. But have you ever heard the story of the Other Wise Man, who also saw the star in its rising, and set out to follow it, yet did not arrive with his brethren in the presence of the young child Jesus? Of the great desire of this fourth pilgrim, and how it was denied, yet accomplished in the denial; of his many wanderings and the probations of his soul; of the long way of his seeking, and the strange way of his finding, the One whom he sought—I would tell the tale as I have heard fragments of it in the Hall of Dreams, in the palace of the Heart of Man.

THE SIGN IN THE SKY

THE STORY OF THE
OTHER WISE MAN

THE SIGN IN THE SKY

In the days when Augustus Cæsar was master
of many kings and Herod reigned in Jerusalem,
there lived in the city of Ecbatana, among the
mountains of Persia, a certain man named
Artaban, the Median. His house stood close
to the outermost of the seven walls which en-
circled the royal treasury. From his roof he
could look over the rising battlements of black
and white and crimson and blue and red and
silver and gold, to the hill where the summer
palace of the Parthian emperors glittered like
a jewel in a sevenfold crown.

Around the dwelling of Artaban spread a
fair garden, a tangle of flowers and fruit trees,

watered by a score of streams descending from
the slopes of Mount Orontes, and made musical
by innumerable birds. But all color was lost
in the soft and odorous darkness of the late
September night, and all sounds were hushed
in the deep charm of its silence, save the plash-
ing of the water, like a voice half sobbing and
half laughing under the shadows. High above
the trees a dim glow of light shone through the
curtained arches of the upper chamber, where
the master of the house was holding council
with his friends.

He stood by the doorway to greet his guests—
a tall, dark man of about forty years, with
brilliant eyes set near together under his broad
brow, and firm lines graven around his fine,
thin lips; the brow of a dreamer and the
mouth of a soldier, a man of sensitive feeling
but inflexible will—one of those who, in whatever age they may live, are born for inward
conflict and a life of quest.

His robe was of pure white wool, thrown
over a tunic of silk; and a white pointed cap,
with long lapels at the sides, rested on his
flowing black hair. It was the dress of the

ancient priesthood of the Magi, called the fire-worshipers.

"Welcome!" he said, in his low, pleasant voice, as one after another entered the room—"welcome, Abdus; peace be with you, Rhodaspes and Tigranes, and with you my father, Abgarus. You are all welcome, and this house grows bright with the joy of your presence."

There were nine of the men, differing widely in age, but alike in the richness of their dress of many-colored silks, and in the massive golden collars around their necks, marking them as Parthian nobles, and the winged circles of gold resting upon their breasts, the sign of the followers of Zoroaster.

They took their places around a small black altar at the end of the room, where a tiny flame was burning. Artaban, standing beside it, and waving a barsom of thin tamarisk branches above the fire, fed it with dry sticks of pine and fragrant oils. Then he began the ancient chant of the Yasna, and the voices of his companions

joined in the beautiful hymn to Ahura-
Mazda:

We worship the Spirit Divine, all wisdom and goodness
    possessing,
Surrounded by Holy Immortals, the givers of bounty
    and blessing,
We joy in the works of His hands, His truth and His
    power confessing.

We praise all the things that are pure, for these are
    His only Creation;
The thoughts that are true, and the words and deeds
    that have won approbation;
These are supported by Him and for these we make
    adoration.

Hear us, O Mazda! Thou livest in truth and in
    heavenly gladness;
Cleanse us from falsehood, and keep us from evil
    and bondage to badness;
Pour out the light and the joy of Thy life on our
    darkness and sadness.

Shine on our gardens and fields, Shine on our
    working and weaving;
Shine on the whole race of man, Believing and
    unbelieving;
  Shine on us now through the night,
  Shine on us now in Thy might,
The flame of our holy love and the song of our worship
    receiving.

The fire rose with the chant, throbbing as if it were made of musical flame, until it cast a bright illumination through the whole apartment, revealing its simplicity and splendor.

The floor was laid with tiles of dark blue veined with white; pilasters of twisted silver stood out against the blue walls; the clear-story of round-arched windows above them was hung with azure silk; the vaulted ceiling was a pavement of sapphires, like the body of heaven in its clearness, sown with silver stars. From the four corners of the roof hung four golden magic-wheels, called the tongues of the gods. At the eastern end, behind the altar, there were two dark-red pillars of porphyry; above them a lintel of the same stone, on which was carved the figure of a winged archer, with his arrow set to the string and his bow drawn.

The doorway between the pillars, which opened upon the terrace of the roof, was covered with a heavy curtain of the color of a ripe pomegranate, embroidered with innumerable golden rays shooting upward from the floor.   In effect the room was like a quiet, starry night, all azure and silver, flushed in the east with rosy promise of the dawn. It was, as the house of a man should be, an expression of the character and spirit of the master.

He turned to his friends when the song was ended, and invited them to be seated on the divan at the western end of the room.

" You have come to-night," said he, looking around the circle, " at my call, as the faithful scholars of Zoroaster, to renew your worship and rekindle your faith in the God of Purity, even as this fire has been rekindled on the altar. We worship not the fire, but Him of whom it is the chosen symbol, because it is the purest of all created things. It speaks to us of one who is Light and Truth. Is it not so, my father?"

" It is well said, my son," answered the venerable Abgarus. " The enlightened are never idolaters. They lift the veil of the form and go into the shrine of the reality, and new light and truth are coming to them continually through the old symbols."

" Hear me, then, my father and my friends," said Artaban, very quietly, " while I tell you of the new light and truth that have come to me through the most ancient of all signs. We

"Hear me, then, my father and my friends, while I tell you of the new light and truth."

have searched the secrets of nature together, and studied the healing virtues of water and fire and the plants. We have read also the books of prophecy in which the future is dimly foretold in words that are hard to understand. But the highest of all learning is the knowledge of the stars. To trace their courses is to untangle the threads of mystery of life from the beginning to the end. If we could follow them perfectly, nothing would be hidden from us. But is not our knowledge of them still incomplete? Are there not many stars still beyond our horizon—lights that are known only to the dwellers in the far southland, among the spice-trees of Punt and the gold-mines of Ophir?"

There was a murmur of assent among the listeners.

"The stars," said Tigranes, "are the thoughts of the Eternal. They are numberless. But the thoughts of man can be counted, like the years of his life. The wisdom of the Magi is the greatest of all wisdoms on earth, because it knows its own ignorance. And that is the secret of power. We keep men always looking and waiting for a new sunrise. But we our--

selves know that the darkness is equal to the light, and that the conflict between them will never be ended."

"That does not satisfy me," answered Artaban, "for, if the waiting must be endless, if there could be no fulfilment of it, then it would not be wisdom to look and wait. We should become like those new teachers of the Greeks, who say that there is no truth, and that the only wise men are those who spend their lives in discovering and exposing the lies that have been believed in the world. But the new sunrise will certainly dawn in the appointed time. Do not our own books tell us that this will come to pass, and that men will see the brightness of a great light?"

"That is true," said the voice of Abgarus; "every faithful disciple of Zoroaster knows the prophecy of the Avesta and carries the word in his heart. 'In that day Sosiosh the Victorious shall arise out of the number of the prophets in the east country. Around him shall shine a mighty brightness, and he shall make life everlasting, incorruptible, and immortal, and the dead shall rise again.'"

"This is a dark saying," said Tigranes, "and it may be that we shall never understand it. It is better to consider the things that are near at hand, and to increase the influence of the Magi in their own country, rather than to look for one who may be a stranger, and to whom we must resign our power."

The others seemed to approve these words. There was a silent feeling of agreement manifest among them; their looks responded with that indefinable expression which always follows when a speaker has uttered the thought that has been slumbering in the hearts of his listeners. But Artaban turned to Abgarus with a glow on his face, and said:

"My father, I have kept this prophecy in the secret place of my soul. Religion without a great hope would be like an altar without a living fire. And now the flame has burned more brightly, and by the light of it I have read other words which also have come from the fountain of Truth, and speak yet more clearly of the rising of the Victorious One in his brightness."

He drew from the breast of his tunic two

small rolls of fine linen, with writing upon them, and unfolded them carefully upon his knee.

"In the years that are lost in the past, long before our fathers came into the land of Babylon, there were wise men in Chaldea, from whom the first of the Magi learned the secret of the heavens. And of these Balaam the son of Beor was one of the mightiest. Hear the words of his prophecy: 'There shall come a star out of Jacob, and a scepter shall arise out of Israel.'"

The lips of Tigranes drew downward with contempt, as he said:

"Judah was a captive by the waters of Babylon, and the sons of Jacob were in bondage to our kings. The tribes of Israel are scattered through the mountains like lost sheep, and from the remnant that dwells in Judea under the yoke of Rome neither star nor scepter shall arise."

"And yet," answered Artaban, "it was the Hebrew Daniel, the mighty searcher of dreams, the counselor of kings, the wise Belteshazzar, who was most honored and beloved of our

great King Cyrus. A prophet of sure things and a reader of the thoughts of God, Daniel proved himself to our people. And these are the words that he wrote." (Artaban read from the second roll:) "'Know, therefore, and understand that from the going forth of the commandment to restore Jerusalem, unto the Anointed One, the Prince, the time shall be seven and threescore and two weeks.'"

"But, my son," said Abgarus, doubtfully, "these are mystical numbers. Who can interpret them, or who can find the key that shall unlock their meaning?"

Artaban answered: "It has been shown to me and to my three companions among the Magi—Caspar, Melchior, and Balthazar. We have searched the ancient tablets of Chaldea and computed the time. It falls in this year. We have studied the sky, and in the spring of the year we saw two of the greatest stars draw near together in the sign of the Fish, which is the house of the Hebrews. We also saw a new star there, which shone for one night and then vanished. Now again the two great planets are meeting. This night is their conjunction. My

three brothers are watching at the ancient
Temple of the Seven Spheres, at Borsippa, in
Babylonia, and I am watching here.   If the
star shines again, they will wait ten days for
me at the temple, and then we will set out together for Jerusalem, to see and worship the
promised one who shall be born King of Israel.
I believe the sign will come. I have made ready
for the journey. I have sold my house and my
possessions, and bought these three jewels—a
sapphire, a ruby, and a pearl—to carry them as
tribute to the King. And I ask you to go with
me on the pilgrimage, that we may have joy
together in finding the Prince who is worthy to
be served."

While he was speaking he thrust his hand
into the inmost fold of his girdle and drew out
three great gems—one blue as a fragment of
the night sky, one redder than a ray of sunrise,
and one as pure as the peak of a snow mountain
at twilight—and laid them on the outspread
linen scrolls before him.

But his friends looked on with strange and
alien eyes. A veil of doubt and mistrust came
over their faces, like a fog creeping up from the

marshes to hide the hills. They glanced at
each other with looks of wonder and pity, as
those who have listened to incredible sayings,
the story of a wild vision, or the proposal of an
impossible enterprise.

At last Tigranes said: "Artaban, this is a
vain dream. It comes from too much looking
upon the stars and the cherishing of lofty
thoughts. It would be wiser to spend the time
in gathering money for the new fire-temple at
Chala. No king will ever rise from the broken
race of Israel, and no end will ever come to the
eternal strife of light and darkness. He who
looks for it is a chaser of shadows. Farewell."

And another said: "Artaban, I have no
knowledge of these things, and my office as
guardian of the royal treasure binds me here.
The quest is not for me. But if thou must follow it, fare thee well."

And another said: "In my house there sleeps
a new bride, and I cannot leave her nor take
her with me on this strange journey. This
quest is not for me. But may thy steps be
prospered wherever thou goest. So farewell."

And another said: "I am ill and unfit for

hardship, but there is a man among my servants whom I will send with thee when thou goest, to bring me word how thou farest."

But Abgarus, the oldest and the one who loved Artaban the best, lingered after the others had gone, and said, gravely: "My son, it may be that the light of truth is in this sign that has appeared in the skies, and then it will surely lead to the Prince and the mighty brightness. Or it may be that it is only a shadow of the light, as Tigranes has said, and then he who follows it will have only a long pilgrimage and an empty search. But it is better to follow even the shadow of the best than to remain content with the worst. And those who would see wonderful things must often be ready to travel alone. I am too old for this journey, but my heart shall be a companion of the pilgrimage day and night, and I shall know the end of thy quest. Go in peace."

So one by one they went out of the azure chamber with its silver stars, and Artaban was left in solitude.

He gathered up the jewels and replaced them in his girdle. For a long time he stood

and watched the flame that flickered and sank upon the altar. Then he crossed the hall, lifted the heavy curtain, and passed out between the dull red pillars of porphyry to the terrace on the roof.

The shiver that thrills through the earth ere she rouses from her night sleep had already begun, and the cool wind that heralds the day-break was drawing downward from the lofty snow-traced ravines of Mount Orontes. Birds, half awakened, crept and chirped among the rustling leaves and the smell of ripened grapes came in brief wafts from the arbors.

Far over the eastern plain a white mist stretched like a lake. But where the distant peak of Zagros serrated the western horizon the sky was clear. Jupiter and Saturn rolled to-gether like drops of lambent flame about to blend in one.

As Artaban watched them, behold! an azure spark was born out of the darkness beneath, rounding itself with purple splendors to a crim-son sphere, and spiring upward through rays of saffron and orange into a point of white radiance. Tiny and infinitely remote, yet per-

fect in every part, it pulsated in the enormous vault as if the three jewels in the Magian's breast had mingled and been transformed into a living heart of light.

He bowed his head. He covered his brow with his hands.

"It is the sign," he said. "The King is coming, and I will go to meet him."

BY THE WATERS OF BABYLON

BY THE WATERS OF BABYLON

All night long Vasda, the swiftest of Artaban's horses, had been waiting, saddled and
bridled, in her stall, pawing the ground im-
patiently and shaking her bit as if she shared
the eagerness of her master's purpose, though
she knew not its meaning.

Before the birds had fully roused to their
strong, high, joyful chant of morning song,
before the white mist had begun to lift lazily
from the plain, the other wise man was in the
saddle, riding swiftly along the highroad,
which skirted the base of Mount Orontes,
westward.

How close, how intimate is the comrade-
ship between a man and his favorite horse
on a long journey. It is a silent, comprehen-
sive friendship, an intercourse beyond the need
of words.

They drink at the same wayside spring,

and sleep under the same guardian stars. They
are conscious together of the subduing spell
of nightfall and the quickening joy of daybreak.
The master shares his evening meal with his
hungry companion, and feels the soft, moist
lips caressing the palm of his hand as they close
over the morsel of bread. In the gray dawn he
is roused from his bivouac by the gentle stir
of a warm, sweet breath over his sleeping face,
and looks up into the eyes of his faithful fellow-
traveler, ready and waiting for the toil of the
day. Surely, unless he is a pagan and an un-
believer, by whatever name he calls upon his
God, he will thank Him for this voiceless sym-
pathy, this dumb affection, and his morning
prayer will embrace a double blessing—God
bless us both, and keep our feet from falling
and our souls from death!

And then, through the keen morning air,
the swift hoofs beat their spirited music along
the road, keeping time to the pulsing of two
hearts that are moved with the same eager
desire—to conquer space, to devour the distance, to attain the goal of the journey.

Artaban must, indeed, ride wisely and well

if he would keep the appointed hour with the other Magi; for the route was a hundred and fifty parasangs, and fifteen was the utmost that he could travel in a day. But he knew Vasda's strength, and pushed forward without anxiety, making the fixed distance every day, though he must travel late into the night, and in the morning long before sunrise.

He passed along the brown slopes of Mount Orontes, furrowed by the rocky courses of a hundred torrents.

He crossed the level plains of the Nisæans, where the famous herds of horses, feeding in the wide pastures, tossed their heads at Vasda's approach and galloped away with a thunder of many hoofs, and flocks of wild birds rose suddenly from the swampy meadows, wheeling in great circles with a shining flutter of innumerable wings and shrill cries of surprise.

He traversed the fertile fields of Concabar, where the dust from the threshing-floors filled the air with a golden mist, half hiding the huge Temple of Astarte with its four hundred pillars.

At Baghistan, among the rich gardens watered by fountains from the rock, he looked up at the mountain thrusting its immense rugged brow out over the road, and saw the figure of King Darius trampling upon his fallen foes, and the proud list of his wars and conquests graven high upon the face of the eternal cliff.

Over many a cold and desolate pass, crawling painfully across the wind-swept shoulders of the hills; down many a black mountain gorge, where the river roared and raced before him like a savage guide; across many a smiling vale, with terraces of yellow limestone full of vines and fruit trees; through the oak groves of Carine and the dark Gates of Zagros, walled in by precipices; into the ancient city of Chala, where the people of Samaria had been kept in captivity long ago; and out again by the mighty portal, riven through the encircling hills, where he saw the image of the High Priest of the Magi sculptured on the wall of rock, with hand uplifted as if to bless the centuries of pilgrims; past the entrance of the narrow defile, filled from end to end with orchards of peaches and figs, through which the river Gyndes foamed down to meet him; over the

broad rice-fields, where the autumnal vapors spread their deathly mists; following along the course of the river, under tremulous shadows of poplar and tamarind, among the lower hills; and out upon the flat plain, where the road ran straight as an arrow through the stubble - fields and parched meadows; past the city of Ctesiphon, where the Parthian emperors reigned, and the vast metropolis of Seleucia which Alexander built; across the swirling floods of Tigris and the many channels of Euphrates, flowing yellow through the corn-lands—Artaban pressed onward until he arrived, at nightfall of the tenth day, beneath the shattered walls of populous Babylon.

Vasda was almost spent, and he would gladly have turned into the city to find rest and refreshment for himself and for her. But he knew that it was three hours' journey yet to the Temple of the Seven Spheres, and he must reach the place by midnight if he would find his comrades waiting. So he did not halt, but rode steadily across the stubble-fields.

A grove of date-palms made an island of

glooms in the pale yellow sea. As she passed into the shadow Vasda slackened her pace, and began to pick her way more carefully.

Near the farther end of the darkness an access of caution seemed to fall upon her. She scented some danger or difficulty; it was not in her heart to fly from it—only to be prepared for it, and to meet it wisely as a good horse should do. The grove was close and silent as the tomb; not a leaf rustled, not a bird sang.

She felt her steps before her delicately, carrying her head low, and sighing now and then with apprehension. At last she gave a quick breath of anxiety and dismay, and stood stock-still, quivering in every muscle, before a dark object in the shadow of the last palm-tree.

Artaban dismounted. The dim starlight revealed the form of a man lying across the road. His humble dress and the outline of his haggard face showed that he was probably one of the poor Hebrew exiles who still dwelt in great numbers in the vicinity. His pallid skin, dry and yellow as parchment, bore the mark of the deadly fever which ravaged the marsh-lands in autumn. The chill of death was in

*The dim starlight revealed
the form of a man lying
across the road.*

his lean hand, and, as Artaban released it, the arm fell back inertly upon the motionless breast.

He turned away with a thought of pity, consigning the body to that strange burial which the Magians deemed most fitting—the funeral of the desert, from which the kites and vultures rise on dark wings, and the beasts of prey slink furtively away, leaving only a heap of white bones in the sand.

But, as he turned, a long, faint, ghostly sigh came from the man's lips. The brown, bony fingers closed convulsively on the hem of the Magian's robe and held him fast.

Artaban's heart leaped to his throat, not with fear, but with a dumb resentment at the importunity of this blind delay.

How could he stay here in the darkness to minister to a dying stranger? What claim had this unknown fragment of human life upon his compassion or his service? If he lingered but for an hour he could hardly reach Borsippa at the appointed time. His companions would think he had given up the journey. They would go without him. He would lose his quest.

But if he went on now, the man would surely die. If he stayed, life might be restored. His spirit throbbed and fluttered with the urgency of the crisis. Should he risk the great reward of his divine faith for the sake of a single deed of human love? Should he turn aside, if only for a moment, from the following of the star, to give a cup of cold water to a poor, perishing Hebrew?

"God of truth and purity," he prayed, "direct me in the holy path, the way of wisdom which only Thou knowest."

Then he turned back to the sick man. Loosening the grasp of his hand, he carried him to a little mound at the foot of the palm-tree.

He unbound the thick folds of the turban
and opened the garment above the sunken
breast. He brought water from one of the small
canals near by, and moistened the sufferer's
brow and mouth. He mingled a draught of one
of those simple but potent remedies which he
carried always in his girdle—for the Magians
were physicians as well as astrologers—and
poured it slowly between the colorless lips.
Hour after hour he labored as only a skilful
healer of disease can do; and, at last, the man's
strength returned; he sat up and looked about
him.

"Who art thou?" he said, in the rude dialect
of the country, "and why hast thou sought me
here to bring back my life?"

"I am Artaban the Magian, of the city of
Ecbatana, and I am going to Jerusalem in
search of one who is to be born King of the
Jews, a great Prince and Deliverer of all men.
I dare not delay any longer upon my journey,
for the caravan that has waited for me may
depart without me. But see, here is all that I
have left of bread and wine, and here is a potion
of healing herbs. When thy strength is restored

thou canst find the dwellings of the Hebrews among the houses of Babylon.''

The Jew raised his trembling hand solemnly to heaven.

''Now may the God of Abraham and Isaac and Jacob bless and prosper the journey of the merciful, and bring him in peace to his desired haven. But stay; I have nothing to give thee in return—only this: that I can tell thee where the Messiah must be sought. For our prophets have said that he should be born not in Jerusalem, but in Bethlehem of Judah. May the Lord bring thee in safety to that place, because thou hast had pity upon the sick.''

It was already long past midnight. Artaban rode in haste, and Vasda, restored by the brief rest, ran eagerly through the silent plain and swam the channels of the river. She put forth the remnant of her strength, and fled over the ground like a gazelle.

But the first beam of the sun sent her shadow before her as she entered upon the final stadium of the journey, and the eyes of Artaban, anxiously scanning the great mound of Nimrod and the Temple of the

Seven Spheres, could discern no trace of his friends.

The many-colored terraces of black and orange and red and yellow and green and blue and white, shattered by the convulsions of nature, and crumbling under the repeated blows of human violence, still glittered like a ruined rainbow in the morning light.

Artaban rode swiftly around the hill. He dismounted and climbed to the highest terrace, looking out toward the west.

The huge desolation of the marshes stretched away to the horizon and the border of the desert. Bitterns stood by the stagnant pools and jackals skulked through the low bushes; but there was no sign of the caravan of the wise men, far or near.

At the edge of the terrace he saw a little cairn of broken bricks, and under them a piece of parchment. He caught it up and read: "We have waited past the midnight and can delay no longer. We go to find the King. Follow us across the desert."

Artaban sat down upon the ground and covered his head in despair.

"How can I cross the desert," said he, "with no food and with a spent horse? I must return to Babylon, sell my sapphire, and buy a train of camels, and provision for the journey. I may never overtake my friends. Only God the merciful knows whether I shall not lose the sight of the King because I tarried to show mercy."

FOR THE SAKE OF A
LITTLE CHILD

FOR THE SAKE OF A LITTLE CHILD

There was a silence in the Hall of Dreams, where I was listening to the story of the Other Wise Man. And through this silence I saw, but very dimly, his figure passing over the dreary undulations of the desert, high upon the back of his camel, rocking steadily onward like a ship over the waves.

The land of death spread its cruel net around him. The stony wastes bore no fruit but briers and thorns. The dark ledges of rock thrust themselves above the surface here and there, like the bones of perished monsters. Arid and inhospitable mountain ranges rose before him, furrowed with dry channels of ancient torrents, white and ghastly as scars on the face of nature. Shifting hills of treacherous sand were heaped like tombs along the horizon. By day,

the fierce heat pressed its intolerable burden on
the quivering air; and no living creature moved
on the dumb, swooning earth but tiny jerboas
scuttling through the parched bushes, or lizards
vanishing in the clefts of the rock. By night
the jackals prowled and barked in the distance,
and the lion made the black ravines echo with
his hollow roaring, while a bitter, blighting
chill followed the fever of the day. Through
heat and cold, the Magian moved steadily
onward.

Then I saw the gardens and orchards of
Damascus, watered by the streams of Aldana
and Pharpar, with their sloping swards inlaid
with bloom, and their thickets of myrrh and
roses. I saw also the long, snowy ridge of Her-
mon, and the dark groves of cedars, and the
valley of the Jordan, and the blue waters of
the Lake of Galilee, and the fertile plain of
Esdraelon and the hills of Ephraim, and the
highlands of Judah. Through all these I followed the figure of Artaban moving steadily
onward, until he arrived at Bethlehem. And it
was the third day after the three wise men had
come to that place and had found Mary and

Joseph, with the young child, Jesus, and had lain their gifts of gold and frankincense and myrrh at his feet.

Then the other wise man drew near, weary, but full of hope, bearing his ruby and his pearl to offer to the King. "For now at last," he said, "I shall surely find him, though it be alone, and later than my brethren. This is the place of which the Hebrew exile told me that the prophets had spoken, and here I shall behold the rising of the great light. But I must inquire about the visit of my brethren, and to what house the star directed them, and to whom they presented their tribute."

The streets of the village seemed to be deserted, and Artaban wondered whether the men had all gone up to the hill-pastures to bring down their sheep. From the open door of a low stone cottage he heard the sound of a woman's voice singing softly. He entered and found a young mother hushing her baby to rest. She told him of the strangers from the Far East who had appeared in the village three days ago, and how they said that a star had guided them to the place where

Joseph of Nazareth was lodging with his wife and her new-born child, and how they had paid reverence to the child and given him many rich gifts.

"But the travelers disappeared again," she continued, "as suddenly as they had come. We were afraid at the strangeness of their visit. We could not understand it. The man of Nazareth took the babe and his mother and fled away that same night secretly, and it was whispered that they were going far away to Egypt. Ever since there has been a spell upon the village; something evil hangs over it. They say that the Roman soldiers are coming from Jerusalem to force a new tax from us, and the men have driven the flocks and herds far back among the hills, and hidden themselves to escape it."

Artaban listened to her gentle, timid speech and the child in her arms looked up in his face and smiled, stretching out its rosy hands to grasp at the winged circle of gold on his breast. His heart warmed to the touch. It seemed like a greeting of love and trust to one who had journeyed long in loneliness and perplexity,

fighting with his own doubts and fears, and following a light that was veiled in clouds.

"Might not this child have been the promised Prince?" he asked within himself, as he touched its soft cheek. "Kings have been born ere now in lowlier houses than this, and the favorite of the stars may rise even from a cottage. But it has not seemed good to the God of wisdom to reward my search so soon and so easily. The one whom I seek has gone before me; and now I must follow the King to Egypt."

The young mother laid the babe in its cradle, and rose to minister to the wants of the strange guest that fate had brought into her house. She set food before him, the plain fare of peasants, but willingly offered, and therefore full of refreshment for the soul as well as for the body. Artaban accepted it gratefully; and, as he ate, the child fell into a happy slumber, and murmured sweetly in its dreams, and a great peace filled the quiet room.

But suddenly there came the noise of a wild confusion and uproar in the streets of the village, a shrieking and wailing of women's voices, a clangor of swords, and a desperate cry: "The soldiers! the soldiers of Herod! They are killing our children."

The young mother's face grew white with terror. She clasped her child to her bosom, and crouched motionless in the darkest corner of the room, covering him with the folds of her robe, lest he should wake and cry.

But Artaban went quickly and stood in the doorway of the house. His broad shoulders filled the portal from side to side, and the peak of his white cap all but touched the lintel.

The soldiers came hurrying down the street with bloody hands and dripping swords. At the sight of the stranger in his imposing dress they hesitated with surprise. The captain of the band approached the threshold to thrust him aside. But Artaban did not stir. His face was as calm as though he were watching the stars, and in his eyes there burned that steady radiance before which even the half-tamed hunting-leopard shrinks and the fierce blood-hound pauses in his leap. He held the soldier silently for an instant, and then said, in a low voice:

"I am all alone in this place, and I am wait-

"I am all alone in this place, and I am waiting to give this jewel to the prudent captain who will leave me in peace."

ing to give this jewel to the prudent captain who will leave me in peace."

He showed the ruby, glistening in the hollow of his hand like a great drop of blood.

The captain was amazed at the splendor of the gem. The pupils of his eyes expanded with desire, and the hard lines of greed wrinkled around his lips. He stretched out his hand and took the ruby.

"March on!" he cried to his men. "There is no child here. The house is still."

The clamor and the clang of arms passed down the street as the headlong fury of the chase sweeps by the secret covert where the trembling deer is hidden. Artaban re-entered the cottage. He turned his face to the east and prayed:

"God of truth, forgive my sin! I have said the thing that is not, to save the life of a child. And two of my gifts are gone. I have spent for man that which was meant for God. Shall I ever be worthy to see the face of the King?"

But the voice of the woman, weeping for joy in the shadow behind him, said, very gently:

"Because thou hast saved the life of my little one, may the Lord bless thee and keep thee; the Lord make His face to shine upon thee and be gracious unto thee; the Lord lift up His countenance upon thee and give thee peace."

IN THE HIDDEN WAY
OF SORROW

IN THE HIDDEN WAY OF SORROW

Then again there was a silence in the Hall of Dreams, deeper and more mysterious than the first interval, and I understood that the years of Artaban were flowing very swiftly under the stillness of that clinging fog, and I caught only a glimpse, here and there, of the river of his life shining through the shadows that concealed its course.

I saw him moving among the throngs of men in populous Egypt, seeking everywhere for traces of the household that had come down from Bethlehem, and finding them under the spreading sycamore-trees of Heliopolis, and beneath the walls of the Roman fortress of New Babylon beside the Nile—traces so faint and dim that they vanished before him continually, as footprints on the hard river-sand glisten for a moment with moisture and then disappear.

I saw him again at the foot of the pyramids,

which lifted their sharp points into the intense saffron glow of the sunset sky, changeless monuments of the perishable glory and the imperishable hope of man. He looked up into the vast countenance of the crouching Sphinx and vainly tried to read the meaning of the calm eyes and smiling mouth. Was it, indeed, the mockery of all effort and all aspiration, as Tigranes had said—the cruel jest of a riddle that has no answer, a search that never can succeed? Or was there a touch of pity and encouragement in that inscrutable smile—a promise that even the defeated should attain a victory, and the disappointed should discover a prize, and the ignorant should be made wise, and the blind should see, and the wandering should come into the haven at last?

I saw him again in an obscure house of Alexandria, taking counsel with a Hebrew rabbi. The venerable man, bending over the rolls of parchment on which the prophecies of Israel were written, read aloud the pathetic words which foretold the sufferings of the promised Messiah—the despised and rejected of men, the man of sorrows and the acquaintance of grief.

"The King whom you are seeking is not to be found in a palace, nor among the rich and powerful."

"And remember, my son," said he, fixing his deep-set eyes upon the face of Artaban, "the King whom you are seeking is not to be found in a palace, nor among the rich and powerful. If the light of the world and the glory of Israel had been appointed to come with the greatness of earthly splendor, it must have appeared long ago. For no son of Abraham will ever again rival the power which Joseph had in the palaces of Egypt, or the magnificence of Solomon throned between the lions in Jerusalem. But the light for which the world is waiting is a new light, the glory that shall rise out of patient and triumphant suffering. And the kingdom which is to be established forever is a new kingdom, the royalty of perfect and unconquerable love.

"I do not know how this shall come to pass, nor how the turbulent kings and peoples of earth shall be brought to acknowledge the Messiah and pay homage to Him. But this I know. Those who seek Him will do well to look among the poor and the lowly, the sorrowful and the oppressed."

So I saw the other wise man again and again,

traveling from place to place, and searching
among the people of the dispersion, with whom
the little family from Bethlehem might, perhaps, have found a refuge. He passed through
countries where famine lay heavy upon the
land, and the poor were crying for bread. He
made his dwelling in plague-stricken cities
where the sick were languishing in the bitter
companionship of helpless misery. He visited
the oppressed and the afflicted in the gloom of
subterranean prisons, and the crowded wretch-
edness of slave-markets, and the weary toil of
galley-ships. In all this populous and intricate
world of anguish, though he found none to
worship, he found many to help. He fed the
hungry, and clothed the naked, and healed the
sick, and comforted the captive; and his years
went by more swiftly than the weaver's shuttle
that flashes back and forth through the loom
while the web grows and the invisible pattern
is completed.

It seemed almost as if he had forgotten his
quest. But once I saw him for a moment as he
stood alone at sunrise, waiting at the gate of a
Roman prison. He had taken from a secret

*In all this populous and intricate world
of anguish, though he found none to
worship, he found many to help.*

resting-place in his bosom the pearl, the last
of his jewels. As he looked at it, a mellower
luster, a soft and iridescent light, full of shifting gleams of azure and rose, trembled upon
its surface. It seemed to have absorbed some
reflection of the colors of the lost sapphire and
ruby. So the profound, secret purpose of a
noble life draws into itself the memories of
past joy and past sorrow. All that has helped
it, all that has hindered it, is transfused by a
subtle magic into its very essence. It becomes
more luminous and precious the longer it is
carried close to the warmth of the beating heart.

Then, at last, while I was thinking of this
pearl, and of its meaning, I heard the end of
the story of the Other Wise Man.

A PEARL OF GREAT PRICE

A PEARL OF GREAT PRICE

Three-and-thirty years of the life of Artaban had passed away, and he was still a pilgrim,
and a seeker after light. His hair, once darker
than the cliffs of Zagros, was now white as
the wintry snow that covered them. His eyes,
that once flashed like flames of fire, were dull
as embers smoldering among the ashes.

Worn and weary and ready to die, but still
looking for the King, he had come for the last
time to Jerusalem. He had often visited the
holy city before, and had searched through all
its lanes and crowded hovels and black prisons
without finding any trace of the family of Naz-
arenes who had fled from Bethlehem long ago.
But now it seemed as if he must make one more
effort, and something whispered in his heart
that, at last, he might succeed.

It was the season of the Passover. The city
was thronged with strangers. The children

of Israel, scattered in far lands all over the
world, had returned to the Temple for the
great feast, and there had been a confusion of
tongues in the narrow streets for many days.

But on this day there was a singular agita-
tion visible in the multitude. The sky was veiled
with a portentous gloom, and currents of excitement seemed to flash through the crowd
like the thrill which shakes the forest on the
eve of a storm. A secret tide was sweeping them
all one way. The clatter of sandals, and the
soft, thick sound of thousands of bare feet
shuffling over the stones, flowed unceasingly
along the street that leads to the Damascus
gate.

Artaban joined company with a group of
people from his own country, Parthian Jews who
had come up to keep the Passover, and inquired
of them the cause of the tumult, and where
they were going.

"We are going," they answered, "to the
place called Golgotha, outside the city walls,
where there is to be an execution. Have you not
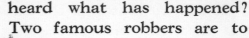
heard what has happened?
Two famous robbers are to

"Pilate has sent him to the cross because he said that he was the 'King of the Jews.'"

be crucified, and with them another, called
Jesus of Nazareth, a man who has done
many wonderful works among the people, so
that they love him greatly. But the priests and
elders have said that he must die, because he
gave himself out to be the Son of God. And
Pilate has sent him to the cross because he
said that he was the 'King of the Jews.'"

How strangely these familiar words fell upon
the tired heart of Artaban! They had led him
for a lifetime over land and sea. And now they
came to him darkly and mysteriously like a
message of despair. The King had arisen, but
He had been denied and cast out. He was about
to perish. Perhaps He was already dying.
Could it be the same who had been born in
Bethlehem thirty-three years ago, at whose
birth the star had appeared in heaven, and of
whose coming the prophets had spoken?

Artaban's heart beat unsteadily with that
troubled, doubtful apprehension which is the
excitement of old age. But he said within himself: "The ways of God are stranger than the
thoughts of men, and it may be that I shall
find the King, at last, in the hands of His ene-

mies, and shall come in time to offer my pearl for His ransom before He dies."

So the old man followed the multitude with slow and painful steps toward the Damascus gate of the city. Just beyond the entrance of the guard-house a troop of Macedonian soldiers came down the street, dragging a young girl with torn dress and disheveled hair. As the Magian paused to look at her with compassion she broke suddenly from the hands of her tormentors and threw herself at his feet, clasping him around the knees. She had seen his white cap and the winged circle on his breast.

"Have pity on me," she cried, "and save me, for the sake of the God of Purity! I also am a daughter of the true religion which is taught by the Magi. My father was a merchant of Parthia, but he is dead, and I am seized for his debts to be sold as a slave. Save me from worse than death."

Artaban trembled.

It was the old conflict in his soul, which had come to him in the palm-grove of Babylon and in the cottage at Bethlehem—the conflict between the ex-

pectation of faith and the impulse of love. Twice the gift which he had consecrated to the worship of religion had been drawn from his hand to the service of humanity. This was the third trial, the ultimate probation, the final and irrevocable choice.

Was it his great opportunity, or his last temptation? He could not tell. One thing only was clear in the darkness of his mind—it was inevitable. And does not the inevitable come from God?

One thing only was sure to his divided heart —to rescue this helpless girl would be a true deed of love. And is not love the light of the soul?

He took the pearl from his bosom. Never had it seemed so luminous, so radiant, so full of tender, living luster. He laid it in the hand of the slave.

"This is thy ransom, daughter! It is the last of my treasures which I kept for the King."

While he spoke, the darkness of the sky thickened, and shuddering tremors ran through the earth, heaving convulsively like the breast of one who struggles with mighty grief.

The walls of the houses rocked to and fro.

Stones were loosened and crashed into the street. Dust-clouds filled the air. The soldiers fled in terror, reeling like drunken men. But Artaban and the girl whom he had ransomed crouched helpless beneath the wall of the Prætorium.

What had he to fear? What had he to live for? He had given away the last remnant of his tribute for the King. He had parted with the last hope of finding Him. The quest was over, and it had failed. But, even in that thought, accepted and embraced, there was peace. It was not resignation. It was not submission. It was something more profound and searching. He knew that all was well, because he had done the best that he could, from day to day. He had been true to the light that had been given to him. He had looked for more. And if he had not found it, if a failure was all that came out of his life, doubtless that was the best that was possible. He had not seen the revelation of "life everlasting, incorruptible, and immortal." But he knew that even if he could live his earthly life over again, it could not be otherwise than it had been.

As she bent over him, fearing that he was dead, there came a voice through the twilight, very small and still, like music sounding from a distance.

One more lingering pulsation of the earth-quake quivered through the ground. A heavy tile, shaken from the roof, fell and struck the old man on the temple. He lay breathless and pale, with his gray head resting on the young girl's shoulder, and the blood trickling from the wound. As she bent over him, fearing that he was dead, there came a voice through the twilight, very small and still, like music sounding from a distance, in which the notes are clear but the words are lost. The girl turned to see if some one had spoken from the window above them, but she saw no one.

Then the old man's lips began to move, as if in answer, and she heard him say in the Parthian tongue:

"Not so, my Lord: For when saw I thee an-hungered and fed thee? Or thirsty, and gave thee drink? When saw I thee a stranger, and took thee in? Or naked, and clothed thee? When saw I thee sick or in prison, and came unto thee? Three-and-thirty years have I looked for thee; but I have never seen thy face, nor ministered to thee, my King."

He ceased, and the sweet voice came again

And again the maid heard it, very faintly and far away. But now it seemed as though she understood the words:

"Verily I say unto thee, Inasmuch as thou hast done it unto one of the least of these my brethren, thou hast done it unto me."

A calm radiance of wonder and joy lighted the pale face of Artaban like the first ray of dawn on a snowy mountain-peak. One long, last breath of relief exhaled gently from his lips.

His journey was ended. His treasures were accepted. The Other Wise Man had found the King.

THE END